Carrie's Table

My Life Through Food

Carrie Jones Faina

AuthorHouse™
1663 Liberty Drive
Bloomington, IN 47403
www.authorhouse.com
Phone: 1 (800) 839-8640

Published by AuthorHouse 05/21/2019

ISBN: 978-1-7283-1193-7 (sc)
ISBN: 978-1-7283-1194-4 (e)

Print information available on the last page.

Any people depicted in stock imagery provided by Getty Images are models,
and such images are being used for illustrative purposes only.
Certain stock imagery © *Getty Images.*

This book is printed on acid-free paper.

authorHOUSE®

In Loving Memory of
Grandpa Robert, Sammy Boy, Albuqurque, and Mischa

Aspirations & Inspirations

i - ii

Introduction

iii - iv

Stories & Recipes

1 - 51

The Menu

Resources & Guides

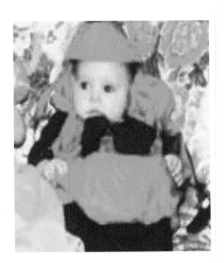

52 - 56

Thank You

57

About the Chef

58

The Menu

"People who love
to eat are always
the best people."

- Julia Child

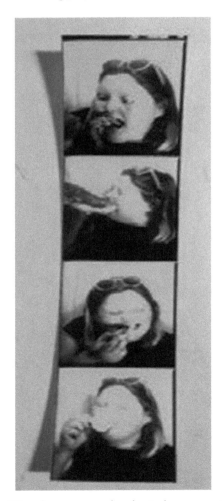

"To deny people their human rights
is to challenge their very humanity"

-Nelson Mandela

"Cooking is all about people. Food is maybe
the only universal thing that really has the power
to bring every- one together. No matter what
culture, everywhere around the world, people get
together to eat."

-Guy Fieri

"Having been in the restaurant business, our job
in the restaurant business is to be responsible
for our customers' happiness. It's the nature of
the hospitality business. You need to take care
of people. You take care of customers above all
others. Customers are your lifeblood."

-Andrew Zimmern

"I always wanted to be a chef. Flavors and food were always of interest to me, but it was how those things brought friends and family together to celebrate not only the special occasions but every-day life. It has been a blessing that I have been able to pursue a career that creates a product that brings people together."

-Maneet Chauhan

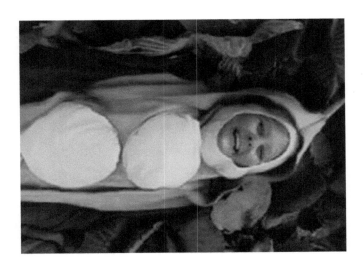

"One cannot think well, love well, sleep well, if one has not dined well."

-Virginia Woolf

The shared meal elevates eating from a mechanical process of fueling the body to a ritual of family and community, from the mere animal biology to an act of culture."

- Michael Pollan

"If you really want to make a friend, go to someone's house and eat with him... the people who give you their food give you their heart."

-Cesar Chavez

"I have the audacity to believe that peoples everywhere can have three meals a day for their bodies, education and culture of their minds, and dignity, equality, and freedom for their spirits

-Martin Luther King Jr.

Introduction

Some of my earliest memories are in the kitchen. For my second birthday, my mom decid-ed to make me a carousel cake. My Grandma Joyce, who always loved to bake and cook, flew in from Idaho to help my mom. My Great Aunt Bev, who lived down the street, came over to help too. Neither Joyce or Bev were good at cooking. They both love to work with food and they try their best but boy are they bad at creating delicious food. I remember one day waking up, not really knowing it was my birthday. There was a sweet aroma in the air traveling throughout the house. Sense of smell is taken for granted. Whether we think about it or not, it is something we learn and memorize. At this age, I had no idea I was smelling cake baking in the oven. Through experience and practice, I have learned that's how cake smells. The sugary, enjoyable scent entering through my nostrils, and entering my little toddler brain knew this was something I wanted to be a part of. Still in my crib, beginning to wake up, I tried to get my mom's attention by "talking" but she couldn't hear me from the kitchen so I began crying. She came to get me and set me up with some toys and a Disney movie in the living room to keep busy while she kept working in the kitchen. I wasn't sat-isfied with the toys. I wanted in on the cake! Everytime I would crawl into the kitchen, Bev, Joyce, or my mom would pick me up and bring me back to the living room. I cried and cried. I tried to explain why I was crying and what I was trying to communicate. In my baby brain, I was speaking perfect English asking, "Can I please help decorate my cake?". I was so frustrated they were not understanding me. No one could figure it out. I could see they were decorating cookies. I saw they were putting icing on the cake. It looked like an art project. I kept thinking "Why won't they let me help?!". I remember being really upset and feeling as if I were purposefully being left out. That's as far as my memory goes for that day. My mom has so many photo albums from my childhood. One of her books has so many pictures of this cake. I don't know if I would have the love for food I have today if I didn't have the privilege of being around the cooking and baking at that young of an age.

This book is full of my introductions to food followed each by three recipes. The first recipe is from my childhood, straight from the story. Then there is an adapted version of the recipe to fit my needs as a teenager, when I had to change my diet due to health complications. The last rec-ipe shown fits the dietary preferences of my current self; these recipes are vegan. This book can be used in many different ways and has no specific order. I hope reading this allows you to pause and think of moments in your life that have influenced your relationship to food.

Recipes & Stories

Wakey Wakey
Eggs and Bakey

Before my sister, Dani and I were born, my mom dreamed of having kids but the man she married, who I used to call dad, was unable to produce quality sperm which would fertilize an egg. They decided to get a sperm donor. Although not biologically related, my sister and I were children to the man my mom was married to, Howard. He was our dad, also known as "King Daddy".

Growing up, I only remember a few breakfasts; french toast, toast with melted American cheese and turkey sausage, milk and cereal, and scrambled eggs. When I was really little, around 3 and 4 years old, before being able to go to school, I would be able to make scrambled eggs with Howard in the kitchen. I'd roll up our kitchen stool and he would allow me to make eggs with him.

King Daddy's

Scrambled Eggs

Ingredients:
3 eggs
¼ C Milk
Salt
Pepper
Canola Oil Spray

1. Beat eggs, milk, salt and pepper with a fork whisk, or a vintage style hand crank egg beater.

2. Spray a medium-sized pan with Pam cooking oil.

3. Heat pan on medium-high heat

4. Add egg mixture to the pan and continue stirring until the mixture turns to solids with no liquid remaining.

5. Serve with loads of ketchup on top.

Queen Carrie's

Veggie Scramble

Ingredients:
4 Egg Whites
1 Large Sausage
1 Handful of
Spinach
1 Red Bell Pepper
Salt
Pepper
Red Pepper Flakes
Canola Oil Spray
Salso

1. Separate eggs and save yolks in an air tight container with a touch of water.

2. Chop pepper and sausage into 1/4 inch pieces.

3. Spray a medium-sized pan with cooking spray.

4. Heat pan on medium-high heat Add egg whites to the pan. When the egg proteins coagulate, stir in other ingredients and season.

5. Serve hot with salsa topping

The Very Best

Chickpea Scramble

Ingredients:
1 Can Chickpeas
1/2 of an Onion
A few cloves of garlic
Sliced mushrooms
Spinach
Salt
Pepper
Garlic powder
Onion Powder
Cumin
Canola Oil Spray

Optional Toppings:
Salsa
Avocado
Chopped Tomatoes
Sriracha
Ketchup

1. Drain chickpeas, transfer to a bowl and mash.

2. Chop onions, mince garlic, and sauté on medium heat until fragrant and translucent.

3. Add mushrooms and sauté until they start to cook down.

4. Add chickpeas to pan. When they start to brown, add seasonings and stir

5. Serve with whichever toppings you please

Family Meetings

I grew up partly culturally Jewish, due to Howard's side of the family, I've become accustomed to bagels and lox. It's a staple in any Jewish family. When my sister, Dani, started having trouble in school my family began having weekly meetings. Howard would come over to our house with a large brown paper bag full of an assortment of bagels: sesame, everything, plain, egg, cinnamon raisin, onion, asiago cheese, pumpernickel, and every other kind of bagel from a Jewish deli. With the bagels, he'd always bring a platter of the fixings. We'd set the platter on the Lazy Susan built into our dining room table and dig into the paper bag, searching for our favorite type of bagel. Mom, Howard, Dani, and I would sit at the table, turning the Lazy Susan, grabbing whatever we wanted to put on our savory donuts. Sitting together over brunch, discussing the week ahead became our ritual over the years. Although our tradition phased out, I continue to eat a bagel for breakfast each Sunday while I go over my calendar for the week.

Jewish Deli

Bagel Breakfast

Go to your local Jewish deli & buy:
A Dozen Bagels, All Types
A Tub of Cream Cheese
Sliced Tomatoes
Sliced Onions
A Container of Capers
½ Pound of Lox

1. Slice your bagel (I prefer an everything bagel).

2. Spread cream cheese on both sides.

3. Add tomato, onions, lox, and capers.

4. Optional: Put the 2 slices together to make a sandwich.

Sleep In Sunday

Bagel with Veggies

Ingredients:
Plain bagels
Avocado
Sliced tomatoes
Salt

1. Slice your bagel.

2. Slice avocado and put on your bagel.

3. Sprinkle salt over the avocado slices.

4. Slice tomato and add to bagel and enjoy.

Green Goddess

Bagel

Ingredients:

For the Bagel:
Everything Bagel
Edamame Hummus
Pesto
Handful of Arugula

For the Edamame Hummus:
1 Cup Cooked Edamame
1 Juiced Lemon
A Drizzle Olive Oil
Enough Water to Blend
A Few Garlic Cloves
Onion Powder
Salt
Pepper

1. Slice your bagel.

2. Blend all hummus ingredients in a blender or food processor. Spread a few tablespoons on bagels.

3. Spread pesto on top of hummus.

4. Top with arugala and cucumbers.

Merry

Christmas Cookin'

For as long as I can remember, my mom has been making granola for all of our family and friends for Christmas presents. As soon as I was old enough, I began helping her with this. Making granola is a pretty tedious task and my mom has grown into not enjoying it as much as she used to. It's tradition and an old family recipe so I guess we keep going with it every year for that reason.

It'll Make You Go Nuts

Christmas Granola

Ingredients:

Dry Ingredients:
4 Cups of Oats
1 Cup Germ Wheat
1/3 - 1/2 Cup Chopped
Almonds
1/3 - 1/2 Cup Chopped
Pecans
1/3 - 1/2 Cup Chopped
Walnuts
1/4 Cup Sunflower Seed
1/2 Cup Pumpkin Seeds

Wet Ingredients
1 Cup Honey
¼ Cup Vegetable Oil
1 teaspoon Vanilla

Add Ins:
Craisins
Raisins

1. Heat oven to 400 degrees F.

2. Measure oats and pour them into a large roasting pan.

3. Chop nuts and add with the rest of the dry ingredients.

4. In a small saucepan, add the honey, oil, and vanilla. Heat to a simmer and stir until a sweet smelling aroma occurs and the ingredients are inseparable.

5. Pour this liquid over the oat mixture and stir.

6. Place in the oven for 1 hour or until golden brown, stirring every 20 minutes.

7. Take out granola and let cool 20 minutes.

8. Stir in add ins.

NutFree

Granola

Ingredients:

Dry Ingredients:
4 Cups of Oats
Wet Ingredients
1 Cup Agave
¼ Cup Coconut Oil
1 teaspoon Vanilla

Add Ins:
Craisins
Raisins

1. Heat oven to 400 degrees F.

2. Measure oats and pour them into a large roasting pan.

3. Mix the dry ingredients.

4. In a small saucepan, melt the honey, oil, and vanilla. Stir.

5. Pour over oats and stir.

6. Place in the oven for 30 minutes to an hour or until golden brown.

HealthNut

Granola

Ingredients:

Dry Ingredients:
2 Cups of Oats
1 Cup Sprouted Buckwheat
1 Cup Puffed Kamut
1/3 Cup Chopped Cashews
1/3 Cup Chopped Almonds
1/4 Cup Pumpkin Seeds
1/4 Cup Sunflower Seeds
1/2 Cup Coconut Chips

Wet Ingredients
¼ Cup Coconut Oil
1 teaspoon Vanilla Extract

1. Heat oven to 400 degrees F.

2. Mix the dry ingredients onto a baking tray.

3. Melt coconut oil and vanilla in a bowl and pour onto the dry ingredients.

4. Place in the oven for 20 minutes for a light toast

Cheviot Hills

Summer Camp

Growing up, I couldn't wait for the school year to end and summer to begin. The day summer would start I would stay at home begging my parents to take me somewhere, anywhere, just to get out of the house and have fun. Every time I'd open my mouth, my mom knew what I was gonna say. The 2 words I knew best during the summertime, I'm sure every parent knows them, the infamous "I'm BOOOORED". There's hardly any getting away from those words when you're a parent. Eventually, my parents began putting me in summer camps. The first summer camp I ever went to was called Cheviot Hills Day Camp. It was for ages 4 to 12 and lasted basically an entire work day, 9 am to 4 pm. We'd have different activities throughout the day like art, cooking, and games. At noon, a few of the camp counselors would go into the office and collect all our lunch boxes into tall rolling bins and bring them out to the grassy picnic area to let all the campers dive into and claim their homemade lunches. I had the same lunch almost everyday, by choice. I'd open up my brown paper lunch bag hoping to find my favorite lunch inside. I would take out each item to display it all in front of me: a plastic bag full of apple slices or a pre-packaged container of carrots and ranch, a plastic water bottle, and a tuna sandwich! I knew the tuna sandwich was my favorite so I'd save that for the last. While all the other campers had lunchables, I was perfectly happy with my simple tuna sandwich.

Tuna-in to This Week's

Sandwich

Ingredients:
1 Can(6-oz) Tuna
1/3 Cup Mayonnaise
A Few Squirts of Lemon
A Pinch of Salt

1. Mix all ingredients except the roll.

2. Refrigerate until cold.

3. Scoop tuna onto the roll and enjoy.

SoFISHticatated Lemon Pepper

Tuna Sandwich

Ingredients:

2 Slices Sesame Ezekial Bread
1 Can(6-oz) Tuna
Juice of 1 Lemon
Lemon Zest of 1/2 a Lemon
1/2 teaspoon of black pepper
1/2 Tablespoon Olive Oil
1 Red Onion
A Handful of Spinach
1 Tomato

1. Cut 2 thin slices of onion and tomato.

2. Mix tuna, lemon, lemon zest, pepper, salt, and olive oil in a small bowl.

3. Toast bread.

4. Top 1 slice of bread with lemon pepper tuna and veggies. Close sandwich with other slice of bread.

TUNAversally Loved Vegan Tuna

Open Faced Sandwich

Ingredients:
2 Rice Cakes
1 (15 oz) Can Chickpeas
1/3 Cup Whole Grain Mustard
2 Celery Sticks
1 Red Onion
1 Small Pickle

1. Drain and mash chickpeas with a fork.

2. Chop veggies into 1/4 inch cubes

3. Mix all ingredients together and top onto rice cakes.

Camp Winnarainbow

The summer going into 5th grade, I remember my sister coming home from her first time away at a sleep away camp in Northern California called Camp Winnarainbow. She came home almost like a new person. She'd learned how to use flower sticks, attempted to juggle, and acquired a new palette. She would ask my mom to make the mac n'cheese she'd had at camp. My mom had no idea how to make it but she kept attempting until Dani gave her the approval. My mom tried all the different combinations of cheeses and pasta she could think of trying to match Dani's brief description. She tried elbow macaroni with Gruyère cheese, parmesan, and cheddar; elbow macaroni with butter, cheddar, and Gorgonzola; elbow macaroni with sharp cheddar, mozzarella, cream, and mustard, and so many other blends. After weeks of trying oodles of noodles, mom finally pleased Dani. Macaroni with Velveeta cheese. It was the most simple recipe imaginable.. So simple she didn't even think of it in the first place. It makes sense now. A child's palette is simple so the recipe must be too. One time the camp kitchen ran out of cheese and had to think on their feet. They threw all the ingredients in the fridge into the pasta and that was the day our new camp lunch tradition, Macabooya was born.

Dani's Begging for
Mac n' Cheese

Ingredients:
Elbow Macaroni
Velveeta Cheese, sliced

1. Cook macaroni according to instructions on the box and drain.

2. While still hot, put a layer of cheese slices on top.

3. On low heat, allow cheese to melt a little, and stir until well combined.

A Circus Favorite
Mac-a-WHATT?!

Ingredients:
1 Box Elbow Macaroni
2 Cups Baby Tomatoes
1/4 Cup Parmesan Cheese
1/4 Cup Pecorino Cheese
3 Tablespoons Parsley
1 Tablespoon Thyme
2 Garlic Chicken Sausages

1. Cook macaroni according to instructions on the box and drain and allow to cool.

2. Slice baby tomatoes in half.

3. Grate the cheeses.

4. Slice sausages into 1/4 inch rounds.

5. Chop herbs and mix all ingredients together, sprinkling cheese in as you mix.

Straight Out of The Garden

Tagliatelle

Ingredients:

1 Package Tagliatelle
2 Chive Blossoms
5 Zucchini Blossoms
1 Zucchini or Yellow Squash
Vegan Parmesan
Olive Oil

1. Cook Tagliatelle according to instructions on the package, drain and allow to cool.

2. Slice zucchini in crescent shapes and sauté.

3. Break chive blossoms into small pieces.

4. Remove center of zucchini blossoms .

5. Drizzle olive oil onto noodles, sprinkle parmesan, tossing in the blossoms and zucchini.

Burned to Perfection

My sister, Dani, and I always loved playing with food. It has always been something we could use to connect with each other. As toddlers, we always played with toy foods, we played with food-based CD-ROM games, and sometimes my mom would even let us cook with her. When it came to Dani and me, my mom always had something fun planned for us. Most of the time she would give us some catalogues and tell us to circle things we wanted. Whenever my sister and I were left alone, even for one second, we would get into some sort of trouble.

We watched our parents cook in the kitchen all the time. We knew we were not allowed to be near the stove, oven, or microwave without one of our parents watching us. We had our own little kitchen we shared. You know, those tiny kitchens people get their kids with the fake stoves, the sink that doesn't have water, and the cupboards that don't actually open. We used that kitchen as if we were 50's house-wives getting ready for a dinner party. It was our favorite spot in the house, besides our playhouse. In our tiny play kitchen, we were allowed to cook anything, using our play food of course. We'd put our chicken drumsticks in the oven, our burgers on the stove, and slide our bread into the toaster. We were basically professional chefs. We had lots of practice baking and decorating food too on our Easy-Bake Kitchen CD CD-ROM Playset. The game was interactive in the way that it was on the computer screen but it also had an attachment connected to the keyboard. The attachment was a miniature kitchen which included an oven, mixer, and egg, measuring cup, roll-ing pin, cutting tool, icing tube, and dough. The whole attachment would clip onto the keyboard and each piece would hit a certain key below which is how your actions could be represented on the screen. On the home screen were a few different options of how you could play. You could click on the jack n the box to play a game, click on the recipe cards to make cool stuff, or the mixing bowl to mess around in the kitchen. Most of the time, Dani and I would click on the mixing bowl. We enjoyed making our own creations. We'd pour the meas-uring cup into the mixing bowl for flour, crack an egg, pour the measuring cup again for wa-ter, then hold down the mixer. Magically, our cake batter would appear in a cake pan. We'd open the oven and on the screen, the cake pan would be placed inside. We had to watch our cake carefully so it didn't burn. The oven on the screen would flash yellow when it was time to take it out. The cake is immediately cooled and brought to the counter to decorate. The oven on the screen would flash yellow when it was time to take it out. The cake is immediate-ly cooled and brought to the counter to decorate. The screen shows four icing tubes on the left of the cake, one for frosting, one for frosting, one for sprinkles and other decorations, and one for writing and candles. There's even a smiling icing tube on the bottom left corner you can click which will give you a completely random design! We'd make cakes, pies, muffins, gingerbread houses and probably some other things. This kept us busy for hours. Or maybe that's just how it felt to us.

One day, my mom was making her favorite family dinner, tuna noodle casserole. Most people hate it, but my family LOVED IT, until we didn't anymore after eating it so often. This was a staple in my childhood. My parents were great parents. They took care of my sister and me and were present all the time until after we went in bed. My mom would go to bed early too so she always chose the fastest, easiest dinners to make. When she would make her tuna casserole she didn't have to think much, she had a routine down. She'd get back home from Von's, our local chain grocery store, with all the ingredients she needed in huge brown paper bags and place them on the floor. She would unload the ingredients onto the kitchen counter, one at a time. She didn't need the recipe in front of her. She knew exactly what to do.

Because we had nothing else going on, my sister and I watched our mom closely as she made the tuna casserole. After putting all of the ingredients in the casserole dish, mom would gently place it in the oven. Dani always had wacky ideas to get us into trou-ble. When mom stepped away from the kitchen for one second, we brought one of our favorite toy foods over towards the oven. This plastic pizza was the most inviting pizza you'd ever seen. It was colorful, with a variety of vegetables on it. Sliced crimini mush-rooms, green and red bell peppers, gorgeous slices of bright red tomatoes, juicy black ol-ives, and lastlysome red onion. It was light and hollow on the inside. Cut into four equal slices with velcro on the sides so we could connect the slices to make a whole pizza. We thought it would be a great idea to warm it up. We saw our mom put food in the oven plenty of times. Why shouldn't we do the same? We slid the pizza into the bottom portion of the oven where we could reach. Unfortunately, this was the broiler. We had one of the older ovens with the top part being the convection oven and the small lower drawer be-ing the broiler; many people use this compartment as storage for their sheet pans now. My mom came running in after smelling the burning plastic. She saw smoke and turned to us, innocent little toddlers playing in the corner and said, "What have you gotten into this time?!" We giggled. She opened the broiler, grabbed metal tongs, and pulled out our pizza. It was nearly still intact. It still looked like a pizza just slightly melted and black on the top. To my sister and me, it was a culinary masterpiece.

Discussing this memory with my mom now, she claims "it was pure, childhood absurdity". She had never laughed so hard in her life. After that day we weren't allowed in the kitch-en for a while. I'm sure that plastic was hard to clean out of the oven. From then on, our parents decided to Dani and I should stick with the Easy Bake Kitchen.

Burned and Melted

Plastic Pizza

Ingredients:

Plastic toy pizza

1. Heat oven on broil.

2. Place plastic toy pizza on bottom rack or closest to heat source.

3. When you begin to see and smell smoke, your pizza is done and your mother will panic!

Pillsbury Dough

Tomato Pizza

Ingredients:

1 tube Pillsbury Pizza Dough
Jar of tomato sauce
Shredded Mozzarella
Large Tomatoes

1. Heat your oven to 425 F.

2. Roll out dough onto a baking sheet.

3. Spread tomato majority of dough, leaving room for crust.

4. Sprinkle a generous amount of cheese.

5. Add tomato slices and bake for about 20 minutes.

Healing Garlic

Tomato Galette

Ingredients:
12 oz Flour
2.5 oz Vegan Butter
2.5 oz Cold Water
0.2 oz Salt
1/2 Cup Cashews
1/2 Cup Vegan Milk
A Few Squirts of Lemon
Fresh Basil
Fresh Rosemary
Salt
Pepper

1. Soak cashews in water 20 minutes to overnight.

2. Heat oven to 375 F. In a large bowl or mixer, add flour, vegan butter, and salt. Slowly add in water. When the dough starts to form, take it out of bowl and knead it with your hands for about 10 minutes.

3. Strain cashews and add to a blender with vegan milk, lemon, garlic, salt, basil, and rosemary.

4. Slice tomatoes and roll out dough, spread cashew garlic mix, add tomatoes. Sprinkle with salt and pepper. Fold dough over. Place in fridge for 20 minutes, then bake for 30 minutes

Rustic Italian

Pizza

Ingredients:
2 kg Flour
250 g Warm Water
200 g Olive Oil
100 g yeast
60 g salt
Your Favorite Pizza Toppings

1. Heat pizza oven (usually gets to around 800 F) or if using conventional oven, heat to the highest tempurature available. Mix yeast in with water, then add olive oil.

2. In a separate bowl, add flour and salt. Slowly start adding the liquid ingredients.

3. When the dough starts to form, knead on flat surface for 15-20 minutes. Roll out dough and add toppings.

4. Gently place pizza in the pizza oven and turn once.

Mama T's

Tuna Noodle Casserole

Ingredients:

1 can tuna

1 can cream of mushroom soup

1/2 onion chopped

2 ribs celery chopped

1 small package egg noodles

1/2 C. frozen peas, thawed

shredded cheese

crushed potato chips

1. Heat oven to 350 F and grease a casserole dish with oil.

2. Cook noodles according to box.

3. In the casserole dish, mix noodles with soup, onion, celery, tuna, and peas.

4. Sprinkle top with cheese and crushed potato chips.

5. Bake about 30 minutes.

Slightly Healthier

Tuna Noodle Casserole

Ingredients:

1 can tuna
1 Cup Mushroom Puree Soup
1/2 onion chopped
2 ribs celery chopped
1 small package egg noodles
1/2 C. frozen peas, thawed

1. Heat your oven to 350 F.

2. Grease a casserole dish with oil.

3. Sauté onions, celery, and peas.

4. Cook noodles according to box.

5. In the casserole dish, mix noodles with mushroom puree soup, tuna, onion, celery, and peas.

6. Bake 45 minutes.

" *They See Me Casse-ROLLIN* "
Chickpea Noodle Casserole

Ingredients:

A spoonful of Vegan Butter
1 Can Chickpeas
A Few Cloves of Garlic
1/2 onion, chopped
2 ribs celery, chopped
1/2 C. Frozen peas, thawed
1/3 Cup Corn
2 Cups Unsweetened Cashew
Milk
2 Tbsp. Flour
1 box of elbow noodles
Store Bought Vegan Cheese or
Cheeze Sauce

Vegan Cheese Sauce:
1 Large Carrot
2 Potatoes
A Few Shakes of Garlic Powder,
Onion Powder, Cayenne, Salt
1/2 Cup Water
1/4 Cup Olive Oil
Juice From 1 Small Lemon
1/4 to 1/2 Cup Nutritional Yeast

Topping:
Dehydrated Onions

1. Heat your oven to 350 F.

2. Grease a casserole dish with oil.

3. Mash the majority of chickpeas.

4. Heat butter in sauté pan on medium heat.

5. Sauté garlic, onions, celery, peas, and corn.

6. Cook noodles until soft but still a tiny bit of resistance to your bite (al dente).

7. If making cheese sauce, boil or steam carrot and potatoes, then blend ingredients together.

8. When the veggies in the pan have softened, add in flour, stirring consistently.

9. Add in cashew milk and bring to a boil until thickened.

10. Add vegan cheese or cheese sauce.

11. Stir in chickpeas and top with dehydrated onions.

12. Bake for 30-40 minutes.

Family Time Watching
Food Network Star

After my parents separated, my mom bought a new home a few miles from Howard to make it easy on my sister and me. We had a set schedule of when we would stay where but after some time, Dani and I were living with mom all the time. Just out of convenience. We still saw Howard everyday. Because Dani was in middle school and extremely social, she was usually on the phone or video chatting her friends with the door to our room locked, leaving me to figure out where to go. Normally, I'd end up in our living room watching tv with my mom. My mom didn't know good tv shows existed yet so we would stick to documentaries, docuseries, and movies. Scrolling through channels, passing cheesy Hallmark movies, bland children shows, and infinite sports channels, we stumbled upon a commercial for season 3 of Next Food Network Star. It intrigued us both so we stopped scrolling through chan-nels and watched. We couldn't take our eyes off. Why hadn't we heard about this show before?! We ran to the kitchen to mark the season premier date on our calendar.

A few months later, the time had come for the first episode. We were so ex-cited! We'd never seen a show quite like this. It was funny, educational, inspiring, and just over all amusing. My mom and I realized it was the first show we could both connect on.

A few episodes in, Dani decided to join us to see what we wouldn't stop talking about. She also fell in love with the show. It was close to impossible for the 3 of us to be in the same room together without Dani and I fighting and my mom feeling upset.

This show brought us together for the first time in a very long time. Twelve years later and we still watch it together.

Chicken

Pot Pie Pockets

Ingredients:

2 Tablespoons Butter
1 Onion
2 Carrots
1 Celery Stick
Salt
Pepper
4 Garlic Cloves
2 Teaspoons Thyme
1 1/2 Tablespoon Flour
1/2 Cup Sherry
1 Cup Chicken Broth
1 Teaspoon Dijon Mustard
1/2 Cup Frozen Peas
1 1/2 Cups Cubed Chicken
1 Sheet Frozen Puff Pastry, thawed
1 Egg

1. Preheat the oven to 375 degrees F.

2. Melt the butter in a large sauté pan over medium heat. Cook the chopped onions, chopped carrots, and chopped celery with salt and pepper, to taste, until the carrots soften. Add the garlic and thyme and cook for a few minutes, stirring frequently.

3. Add the flour and cook about 1 minute. Turn heat to medium-high, pour in sherry and stir slowly, getting all the flour and veggies of the bottom of the pan. Whisk in the broth and mustard.

4. Stir in the peas and chicken. Cook on low until sauce thickens.

5. Remove from heat and set aside.

6. Flour a flat surface and unfold the puff pastry. Cut down the middle vertically and horizontally, making 4 squares. Flour a rolling pin and roll out the squares. Put them on a baking sheet and scoop the filling in the center. Fold the squares to make triangle. Seal the ends together by pinching together (wet your fingertips with water if they're having trouble sticking). Whisk the egg with a splash of water and brush over the pot pie pockets. Cut a small line on each pocket to allow them to steam. Bake about 30 minutes or until golden brown. Stand about 10 minutes to cool.

Chicken and Biscuits

Ingredients:

Filling:
4 Tablespoons Butter
2 Cups Mirepoix
1/3 Cup Flour
1 1/2 Cups Chicken Stock
1 1/2 Cups Milk
1/2 Teaspoon Dried Sage
1/2 Teaspoon Dried Thyme
2 Cups Diced Cooked Chicken
1/2 Cups Cooked Peas
1/2 Cup Corn
Salt
Pepper

Biscuit Topping:
2 Cups Flour
1 Tablespoon Baking Powder
1/2 Teaspoon Salt
3/4 Cup Milk
8 (1 inch) Pieces Cold Butter

1. On medium heat, melt the butter for the large oven safe pot. Stir in the mirepoix. Cover and cook for 7 to 8 minutes, stirring every so often. Then stir in flour.

2. Whisk the stock into the pan. As it begins to thicken, whisk in the milk. Add the herbs and veggies. Cook and stir for another 5 to 7 minutes. Add salt.

3. Remove the pan from heat. Heat oven to 375 F. While the oven heats, make the biscuits by combining the dry ingredients together. Use your fingertips to rub the butter, incorporating it into the dry ingredients. Pour in the milk and stir just until the dough forms

4. Put the dough on a floured surface, kneading it for a couple minutes. Shape the dough into a 1/2 inch thick disk.. Using a small cookie cutter cut out circles and put as many as can fit in the pot as possible with out touching.

5. Bake until the biscuits golden brown and the filling boils, about half an hour. Allow to cool 10 minutes.

Let's Begin the Vegan

Mini Pot Pies

Ingredients:

For Filling:
3 Garlic Cloves
1 Yellow Onion
2 1/2 Cups Vegetable Broth
2 Carrots
1 Cup Corn
3/4 Cup Peas
A Couple Yukon Gold and
Russet Potatoes
1/2 Cup Plant Based Milk
A Few Sprigs of Thyme
3/4 Cup + 2 Tablespoons
Flour

For Crust:
1/2 Cup + 2 Tablespoons
Cold Plant Based Butter
3-7 Tablespoons Cold Water
1 1/2 Cups Flour
A Pinch of Salt

1. First, make the crust. A food processor is great for this but a large mixing bowl with a fork, two knives, or pastry blender will work too. Stir flour and salt then add in small pieces of butter and pulse/cut in the butter quickly so it doesn't melt. You want the flour to combine with the butter to make little balls the size of green peas.

2. Mix in cold water one tablespoon at a time, only enough to help the dough come together. Using your hands, knead the dough on a floured surface and roll into a smooth ball of dough. Wrap in cling wrap, bees wax paper, or put the dough in a bowl and cover with a silicone bowl cover or a plate. Store in the fridge for later.

3. Preheat the oven to 425 degrees F and prepare 5 or 6 ramekin dishes on a baking sheet.

4. Mince garlic and chop vegetables, the potatoes quartered. Heat a large skillet on medium-high heat and sauté olive oil, garlic and onion.

5. Once the onion and garlic are fragrant and translucent Add flour and stir quickly. Gradually stir in vegetable broth and then the plant based milk.

6. Simmer until thickened. If too thick, add more broth. If too thin, take out a little liquid and add a couple tablespoons of flour.

7. When the sauce thickens (you can test this by gliding the back of a spoon over the sauce and seeing if it sticks), add in other vegetables and add salt and thyme. Sauté for 5-10 minutes.

8. On a well floured surface, roll out the dough and cut out circles using one of the ramekins.

9. Fill the ramekins with the pot pie filling and cover with the dough cut outs.

Children Run
Restaurant

When I was little, my sister Dani, my best friend Melanie, her brother Dus-tin, and I would often invite our parents to eat a meal at our restaurant and see our band perform live. Although all of us considered ourselves chefs, we didn't know about the different roles in a restaurant. Despite that, we unknowingly took on standard roles. Since Dustin was the oldest, he was automatically the manager. My sister was the hostess and server, and Melanie and I were servers. We'd run around from the living room to the kitchen completing all the different jobs we assigned ourselves. Most res-taurants take months if not years to open up. Ours took less than a full day.

We'd set up the dining room to look super fancy, or so we thought. It took us all day to come up with a cohesive list of dishes that would work well together and foods we could actually make. In the end, none of the dishes really fit together but we made it work somehow. And we would spend all day creating individual menus for each 'customer'. With all our crayons spread all over the floor and white printer paper scattered everywhere, we would hand write each menu which also included drawings of each dish. The menus usually ended up being peanut butter and jelly sandwiches, mac n' cheese, and a pudding cup for dessert. Silly things like that. When the menus were done, the four of us would all congregate in the kitchen and prepare our specials dishes. Since we couldn't see over the counter, each of us had to pull up stools to stand on. Dustin would make grilled PB&Js, Dani would make microwavable mac n' cheese, sometimes cup noodles, Melanie made Lunchables pizzas, and I would often microwave Campbell's tomato soup and rip up some pieces of a head of lettuce to garnish the soup.

We served these dishes one by one to our parents. They took so long to eat each dish. I wonder why. Older people always take a long time at meals. After they finally finished eating their main courses, we would bring out the dessert. We loved to serve the "Carrie and Dani Special" which was a parfait created by yours truly. We had these tall, "fancy" plastic cups which were only used in our house to make this specific dessert. We'd grab one of those and dish up. First, at the bottom of the cup was a few spoonfuls of chocolate pudding, then a layer of whip cream, then some jiggly red jello. We'd repeat these layers a couple times until it got close to the top of the cup. When it reached close to the top, we'd put one last layer of whip cream and top it off with a strawberry. We thought this was the best thing. As the desserts were being served, we'd set up for our live show. Just recently I was told how gross these dinners were but we didn't know. We had little baby untrained palettes.

Shredded Lettuce Topped in

Tomato Soup

Ingredients:

1 Can Cream of Tomato Soup
Head of Lettuce

1. Heat soup in the microwave.

2. Using your hands, tear lettuce into uneven pieces and top soup before serving.

Grilled Cheese Sandwiches with

Tomato Soup

Ingredients:

For the Soup:
6 Large Tomatoes
About 1 Cup Vegetable Broth
A Few Basil Leaves
A Few Cloves of Garlic
Olive Oil
Salt
Pepper

For Grilled Cheeses
2 Slices Whole Wheat Bread
2 Squares American Cheese
Butter

1. Heat oven to 400 F.

2. Slice tomatoes and garlic cloves in half. Remove the sprout in the center of the garlic. Place on a baking sheet. Drizzle with olive oil and sprinkle salt and pepper.

3. Roast garlic and tomatoes in oven until the tomatoes have a dark caramelization.

4. Place all ingredients in a blender or use an immersion blender. Blend to desired consistency.

5. Spread butter on one side of each slice of bread. Add cheese to non-buttered side of bread. Top with other slice. The buttery side will be on the outside. Grill each side.

Secretly Vegetable Filled

Tomato Soup

Ingredients:

2 Medium Sized Carrots
1 Zucchini
1 Yellow Squash
3 Roma Tomatoes
1 Large Yellow Onion
5 Cloves of Garlic
1 /2 Box of Vegetable Broth

1. Chop all vegetables and mince garlic.

2. Sauté onions. When onions are fragrant and translucent, add garlic.

3. Once the garlic is golden brown, add carrots until they begin to soften.

4. Add in zucchini and squash. Cook down all vegetables and then add the tomatoes and broth, let simmer.

5. If desired, take out half the soup and put in another container. Using an immersion blender or a kitchen blender, (immersion blenders come in handy here) blend half the soup. Add the other half back in with the blended half.

6. Serve warm.

Growing Up On

Weight Watchers

A pretty big portion of my childhood, I was eating Weight Watchers food. My mom was always going on and off Weight Watchers. One of her favorite and easiest recipes she learned how to make was black bean soup. My sister and I never really understood why we had to eat such a boring soup but it's un-derstandable now.

Weight Watchers

Black Bean Soup

Ingredients:
1 onion, chopped
Chicken Broth
4 cans black beans
1 Small Jar of Salsa
Chili Powder
1 Small Container of Sour Cream

1. Spray saucepan with cooking spray.

2. Sauté onions until soft.

3. Add salsa, chicken broth and 3 cans black beans. Add chili powder to taste.

4. Simmer for about half an hour or more.

5. Blend soup until smooth.

6. Return to pot, add remaining can of beans.

7. Stir in sour cream and simmer for a few minutes.

Quesidillas with

Black Bean Soup

Ingredients:

For the Soup:
1 Onion
2 Garlic Cloves
2 Handfuls Baby Tomatoes
4 Cans of Black Beans
1/3 Box of Vegetable Broth

For Quesadilla:
Flour Tortillas
Mexican Cheese Mix

1. Mince garlic, chop onion.

2. Sauté onions until soft. Add garlic.

3. Add black beans and broth.

4. Simmer for 25-30 minutes.

5. Heat tortilla on a separate pan.

6. Add cheese to half of the tortilla and fold.

7. Flip the quesadilla to get both sides toasted.

I'm Sick of

Black Bean Soup

Ingredients:

Olive Oil
1 Roma Tomato
2 Garlic Cloves
1 Onion
1 Carrot
2 Ribs of Celery
4 Cups Cooked Beans
3 Cups Vegetable Broth
Fresh Sage
Fresh Thyme
Fresh Rosemary

1. Mince garlic and finely chop the vegetables with olive oil and cook in a pot until translucent and soft.

2. Add beans, broth, herbs and salt to taste. Stir together, simmer for 45 minutes-1 hour.

3. Puree the beans in batches in a food mill.

4. Serve with a drizzle of olive oil and finely diced tomatoes.

Dinner for
Luke

My mom always wanted my sister and me to be musical. She grew up in a musical family who would gather around the piano and sing songs together. She was always involved in musical theater and wanted the same for Dani and me. It gave her an outlet and a sense of being. It also gave her a connection to others. While Dani felt that about music too, one thing all of us agreed on was the connection of food.

My mom always had us signed up for activities. When I was about 7 or 8 years old, Dani and I began taking piano lessons at The Music Castle. At first, we would drive there for our lessons with our teacher Luke. We would be there for hours at a time. It felt like the entire family had lessons. Mom, Dani, me, and our family friend Omar. We would all fight over who would go first. No one wanted to. It was the same feeling you have when someone watches you type. The feeling of getting something wrong and feeling judged within an instant. That's what it was for me anyway. Luke was the nicest guy and was not judge-mental at all, so it was probably just me being hard on myself. I did sometimes feel like he felt like we were wasting his time a little. We just played around with him and most of the time he would join in on it but other times you could tell he wasn't feeling" it. We would have Luke to listen to a song on and play it on the piano right afterward, we'd ask him about what he had for lunch, we'd steal his sour tangerine Altoids. We probably took all his money in Altoids. We never even practiced outside of our lessons so we never improved. So I don't blame him if he did feel annoyed at times.

Over time, as we became comfortable, he came to our house for lessons. We played the same kinda games with him when he came to our house. Dur-ing our lessons, my mom and Omar's mom would make dinner and when we all finished our lessons, we'd invite Luke to eat dinner with us. One time we had enchiladas for dinner and Luke absolutely fell in love with them. From then on we made enchiladas every time Luke came over.

Luke's Favorite

Chicken Enchiladas

Ingredients:

Chicken Breasts, Cooked and Shredded
1 Package of Tortillas
1/2 of an Onion, Chopped
1 Can Green Chiles, 4.5 oz
1 Can Green Enchilada Sauce, 28 oz
Shredded Cheese

1. Spray a casserole dish with Pam Cooking Spray and heat oven to 350 F.

2. In a large bowl, mix chicken, onion, green chiles, 1/3 cup enchilada sauce, and a sprinkle of cheese.

3. If using corn tortillas, soften them by heating on a pan.

4. Put a few tablespoons of the chicken mixture in a tortilla, roll tightly, and place in the casserole dish. Repeat until dish is full.

5. Pour enchilada sauce over enchiladas and sprinkle cheese to cover the top.

6. Bake 30 minutes. Serve with sour cream, salsa, lettuce, rice, and beans.

Black Bean and Corn

Enchiladas

Ingredients:
1 Can Black Beans, 15.5 oz
1 Jar Corn and Chile Salsa
8 Flour Tortillas
1 Can Red Enchilada
Sauce, 28 oz
Shredded Cheese
Cilantro

1. Spray a casserole dish with Pam Cooking spray and heat oven to 350 F.

2. In an assembly line, take a tortilla then add beans, then corn salsa, and roll. Place in the casserole dish. Repeat with the other seven tortillas.

3. Pour enchilada sauce over enchiladas and sprinkle cheese on top.

4. Bake 30 minutes or until the cheese has melted.

5. Top with cilantro. Serve with salsa, guacamole, lettuce, and beans.

Farm Fresh

Enchiladas

Ingredients:
Olive Oil
1 Garlic Bulb
1 Zucchini
6 Pattypan Squash
1 Red Bell Pepper
1 Green Bell Pepper
1/2 White Onion
1/2 Red Onion
2 Ears of Corn
1 Bunch
1 Cup Brussels Sprouts
1 1/2 Cups Cooked Lentils
1 Jicama
2 Avocados
2 Limes
2 Tablespoons Fresh Cilantro
1 Can Red Enchilada
Sauce, 28 oz

1. Preheat oven to 350 F.

2. Chop all veggies and cook lentils.

3. Roast or sauté vegetables with the head of garlic, olive oil, salt, and pepper.

4. While the vegetables cook, chop jicama into 1/2 inch cubes and chop cilantro.

5. When vegetables begin to soften and lentils are cooked but still slightly firm, you can begin filling the tortillas. A generous helping of veggies, a couple tablespoons of lentils, and drizzle of enchilada sauce. Roll, and place in a baking dish. Continue until dish is full. Cover with enchilada sauce.

6. Place in the oven for 20-30 minutes.

7. Meanwhile, make the avacado, jicama topping by cutting the avocados into 1/2 inch cubes and mixing with the jicama. Mix with fresh lime juice and chopped cilantro.

Carrie the
Foodventurist

When I was a kid Howard would take Dani and me on Daddy-Daughter trips. We were fortunate enough to take these trips once a year. One year we spent a week in Hawaii. We stayed on the island of Honolulu at a gorgeous pink hotel right on the ocean. Dani and I were able to run around on our own, going from the beach to the pool and even the mall. We ran around in our bathing suits, as little kids do before society tells you that it isn't acceptable. We didn't know it at the time but these trips were actually business trips for Howard. We would go out to breakfast, get a loco moco with a side of Portu-guese sausage from The Rainbow Drive-In, hike to Waimea Falls, and go back to the hotel room for a rest. While Dani and I went swimming, Howard would take a few hours for business calls. When we'd come back from the pool and realize he was still on the phone we would be so annoyed but we would still wait patiently for him to be done. Once he hung up from the last phone call, it was time for dinner. This is what a typical Daddy-Daughter trip looked like. Howard would always decide what we got for dinner. And one night, he felt like sushi. I'd never had sushi before. Neither had Dani. I was a little hesitant but excited to try this new food. Knowing it was raw fish freaked me out a little but what 8-year-old wouldn't be. Dani was so against trying it, we decid-ed to stop and get her a hamburger on the way. We pulled up to a little black building with a huge sign which read "Sushi Sasabune! Trust Me!". We were brought to a table. Howard and I were excited and Dani had a burger in hand. We sat down and I told Howard to order for me. I trusted him with all my heart. I don't remember the first dish that I tasted but I do remember feeling welcomed to a whole new world. My face lit up like Disneyland's Main Street. The look of fish but the taste of candy lingering over my taste buds. Who knew fish could literally, and I mean literally, melt in your mouth.

From that first bite, I was hooked. Dani, still munching on her hamburger, seemed pretty amused but did not want to try some herself. At Sasabune, when you order the Trust Me, you're ordering the 10 best sushi rolls and sashimi dishes recommended by the chef. The meal always ends with the best of the best. Since I was a tiny tot this was my motto: save the best for last. After you finish the other servings, you are brought a fragile, warm, delicately wrapped blue crab hand roll. I remember Howard instructing me to not wait for his roll to come and that I must eat it right away, while it is still warm so the nori didn't lose its quality. If you let it sit, even for 30 seconds, the nori will get warm, start to shrivel and become soggy, losing all its flavor and crisp texture. I grabbed the roll with my little hands and took a big ol' bite. My eyes shut slowly like a young child being sung to sleep. I was in a dream world. I scarfed that thing down so fast. All of a sudden, it was gone. And we had to leave. I was devastated we were done with our meal. I'll never forget the feeling I had with my first bite of that dreamy, creamy hand roll. I'll think about it for the rest of time.

Blue Crab Hand Roll

Go to Sasabune and Order:
The Trust Me

1. Go to Sushi Sasabune and wait for a table.

2. When seated, ask for the Trust Me. Chef Kazunori Nozawa has curated this special menu, honoring the traditional Japanese Omakase style sushi which lets the fish be the star of the dish rather than adding tons of vegetables and toppings.

3. You will be brought a number of different dishes starting with Edamame, then Tuna Sashimi, Albacore Sushi, Salmon Sushi, Toro Hand Roll, Yellowtail Sushi, followed by the Sea Bass Sushi, and then before your very eyes, the most gorgeous, precious sushi roll you've ever seen in your life. The Blue Crab Hand Roll.

Spring Time

Asian Salmon Dinner

Ingredients:

**1 Tablespoon Wasabi
Powder
2 Tablespoons Water
1 1/4 Cup Ponzu Sauce
1/4 Cup Sake
2 Tablespoons Fresh Ginger
3 (1/4 lb) Pieces Salmon Fillet
1 Bunch Broccolini
2 Tablespoons Oil
1 Tablespoon Sesame Seeds
3 Cups Warm Cooked Rice
2 Teaspoons Sesame Oil
3 Green Onions, Chopped
1 Avocado, Cubed
1 Cucumber, Julienned
1/4 Cup Sliced Pickled Ginger**

1. Start by combining the wasabi powder and water in a saucepan and let sit a few minutes. Bring sake, ginger, and 3/4 cup ponzu to a boil. Simmer on medium-low heat for about 10 minutes until sauce reduces and thickens (test if it coats the back of a spoon).

2. Marinate the salmon and broccolini in the rest of the ponzu sause and oil for 10 minutes.

3. Toast the sesame seeds on the stove until fragrant. Pour directly onto a plate and let cool. Heat a grill pan on medium heat until. Remove the broccolini from the marinate and cook on the grill pan a few minutes. Place a plate and cover with tin foil, shiny side down, to keep warm. Put the salmon on the grill pan, cooking 2 to 3 minutes on each side.

4. Assemble the meal in a few bowls. Add the rice to the bottom and place the salmon, broccolini, and cucumbers on top. Pour the sauce over and top with sesame seeds, green onions, avocado, and pickled ginger.

Vegan

Tomato "Poke" Bowl

Ingredients:

For the Poke:
2 Heirloom Tomatoes
Sesame Oil
Soy Sauce

For the Bowl:
3 Different Types Radishes
¼ of a Medium-Sized Cucumber
1 Cup of Pickled Vegetables
¼ Cup Sliced Mushrooms
¼ Cup Edamame
1 Cup Dry Wild Rice 3Cups Vegetable Broth
½ Cup Dinosaur Kale
Sesame Seeds

1. For the Poke: Dice the tomatoes into ¼ inch cubes. Place into a container. Drizzle sesame oil and soy sauce. Toss. Let sit for at least 1 hour

2. For the Bowl: In a medium-size pot, heat the vegetable stock on medium-high heat until it comes to a boil.

3. Once boiling, add rice and lower heat to medium-low. Put the top on the pot and let cook until the stock is absorbed into the rice. When rice is soft, fluff with a fork.

4. Slice the mushrooms in ¼ slices.

5. Heat a pan on medium-low heat and add mushrooms, stirring occasionally, letting them brown and expel juices.

6. While the rice and mushrooms are cooking, start to slice the vegetables. You can use a mandolin or a knife for this.

7. For the radishes, slice as thin as possible.

8. For the cucumber, slice diagonally in ¼ slices.

9. Grab a few kale leaves, massage them to bring the flavor out and reduce the bitter flavor, and slice into slivers.

10. When rice and mushrooms are done, you're ready to assemble the bowl.

11. In a salad bowl add your rice. Top with kale, arrange vegetables, and tomato poke. Sprinkle on sesame seeds.

Resources & Guides

Books

Ahmed, Sara. The Promise of Happiness. Duke University Press Books, 2010.

Berrymore, Drew. Wildflower. Penguin Publishing Group, 2015.

Erik, Marcus. The Ultimate Vegan Guide : Erik Marcus : 9781461088011. 2nd ed., CreateSpace Publishing, 2011.

Fiese, Barbara H., and Marlene Schwartz. Reclaiming the Family Table: Mealtimes and Child Health and Wellbeing. Social Policy Report. Volume 22, Number 4. Society for Research in Child Development, 2008. ERIC, https://eric.ed.gov/?id=ED521697.

Foundation, James Beard, et al. Waste Not: How To Get The Most From Your Food. Rizzoli, 2018.

Haidt, Jonathan. The Happiness Hypothesis: Finding Modern Truth in Ancient Wisdom|Paperback. Basic Books, 2006.

Harper, A. Breeze, and Patrice Jones. Sistah Vegan: Black Female Vegans Speak on Food, Identity, Health, and Society: Lantern Books, 2009.

Moran, Victoria. The Love-Powered Diet: Eating for Freedom, Health, and Joy. Lantern Books, 2009.

Nickerson, Brittany Wood. Recipes from the Herbalist's Kitchen: Delicious, Nourishing Food for Lifelong Health and Well-Being. Storey Publishing, LLC, 2017

Penniman, Leah, and Karen Washington. Farming While Black: Soul Fire Farm's Practical Guide to Liberation on the Land: Chelsea Green Publishing, 2018.

Sherman, Sean, and Beth Dooley. The Sioux Chef's Indigenous Kitchen. 1 edition, Univ Of Minnesota Press, 2017.

Thug Kitchen. Thug Kitchen: Eat Like You Give A F**K. Potter/Ten Speed/Harmony/Rodale, 2014.

Winfrey, Oprah. Food, Health, and Happiness: 115 On-Point Recipes for Great Meals and a Better Life. 1 edition, Flatiron Books, 2017.

Films

Bird, Brad. Ratatouille. 2007.

Gelb, David. Jiro Dreams of Sushi. 2012.

Kye, Nari, et al. Wasted! The Story of Food Waste. 2017.

Levy, Joseph. Spinning Plates. 2015.

Rawal, Sanjay. Food Chains. 2014.

Journal Articles

Algert, Susan J., et al. "Disparities in Access to Fresh Produce in Low-Income Neighborhoods in Los Angeles." American Journal of Preventive Medicine, vol. 30, no. 5, May 2006, pp. 365–70. ScienceDirect, doi:10.1016/j.amepre.2006.01.009.

Ares, Gastón, et al. "Food and Wellbeing. Towards a Consumer-Based Approach." Appetite, vol. 74, Mar. 2014, pp. 61–69. ScienceDirect, doi:10.1016/j.appet.2013.11.017.

Beezhold, Bonnie, et al. "Vegans Report Less Stress and Anxiety than Omnivores." Nutritional Neuroscience, vol. 18, no. 7, Oct. 2015, pp. 289–96. EBSCOhost, doi:10.1179/147683051 4Y.0000000164.

Blades, Mabel. "Food and Happiness." Nutrition & Food Science, vol. 39, no. 4, July 2006, pp. 449–54. www-emeraldinsight-com.proxy2.hampshire.edu (Atypon), doi:10.1108/00346650910976310.

Block, Jason P., et al. "Fast Food, Race/Ethnicity, and Income: A Geographic Analysis." American Journal of Preventive Medicine, vol. 27, no. 3, Oct. 2004, pp. 211–17. ScienceDirect, doi:10.1016/j.amepre.2004.06.007.

Casey, Alicia A., et al. "Impact of the Food Environment and Physical Activity Environment on Behaviors and Weight Status in Rural U.S. Communities." Preventive Medicine, vol. 47, no. 6, Dec. 2008, pp. 600–04. PubMed, doi:10.1016/j.ypmed.2008.10.001.

Costanza, Robert, et al. "Quality of Life: An Approach Integrating Opportunities, Human Needs, and Subjective Well-Being." Ecological Economics, vol. 61, no. 2, Mar. 2007, pp. 267–76. ScienceDirect, doi:10.1016/j.ecolecon.2006.02.023.

Craig, Winston J. "Health Effects of Vegan Diets." The American Journal of Clinical Nutrition, vol. 89, no. 5, May 2009, pp. 1627S-1633S. ajcn.nutrition.org, doi:10.3945/ajcn.2009.26736N.

Donohoe, Martin. "Flowers, Diamonds, and Gold: The Destructive Public Health, Human Rights, and Environmental Consequences of Symbols of Love." Human Rights Quarterly. www. academia. edu, https://www.academia.edu/26650386/Flowers_Diamonds_and_Gold_The_ Destructive_Public_Health_Human_Rights_and_Environmental_Consequences_of_Sym bols_of_Love. Accessed 22 Mar. 2019.

Esch, Tobias, and George B. Stefano. "The Neurobiology of Love." Neuro. Endocrinol. Lett, 2005, pp. 175–192.

Frank, L., et al. "Food Outlet Visits, Physical Activity and Body Weight: Variations by Gender and Race–Ethnicity." British Journal of Sports Medicine, vol. 43, no. 2, Feb. 2009, pp. 124–31. bjsm.bmj.com, doi:10.1136/bjsm.2008.055533.

Gottlieb, Robert, and Andrew Fisher. "Community Food Security and Environmental Justice: Searching for a Common Discourse." Agriculture and Human Values, vol. 13, no. 3, June 1996, pp. 23–32. link.springer.com, doi:10.1007/BF01538224.

Hall, Kevin, et al. "The Progressive Increase of Food Waste in America and Its Environmental Impact." PLoS ONE, Vol 4, Iss 11, p E7940 (2009), no. 11, 2009, p. e7940. EBSCOhost, doi:10.1371/journal.pone.0007940.

Howden, S. Mark, et al. "Adapting Agriculture to Climate Change." Proceedings of the National Academy of Sciences, vol. 104, no. 50, Dec. 2007, pp. 19691–96. www.pnas.org, doi:10.1073/pnas.0701890104.

Hunt, Geoffrey, et al. "FOOD IN THE FAMILY: BRINGING YOUNG PEOPLE BACK IN." Appetite, vol. 56, no. 2, Apr. 2011, pp. 394–402. PubMed Central, doi:10.1016/j.appet.2011.01.001.

Johnson, Mark. "Love Promotes Health." Neuroendocrinol Lett. www.academia.edu, https://www.academia.edu/655434/Love_promotes_health. Accessed 22 Mar. 2019.

Karp, Angela, and Goetz M. Richter. "Meeting the Challenge of Food and Energy Security." Journal of Experimental Botany, vol. 62, no. 10, June 2011, pp. 3263–71. academic.oup.com, doi:10.1093/jxb/err099.

Koneswaran, Gowri, and Danielle Nierenberg. "Global Farm Animal Production and Global Warming: Impacting and Mitigating Climate Change." Environmental Health Perspectives, vol. 116, no. 5, May 2008, pp. 578–82.

O'Mara, F. p. "The Significance of Livestock as a Contributor to Global Greenhouse Gas Emissions Today and in the near Future." Animal Feed Science and Technology, vol. 166–167, June 2011, pp. 7–15. EBSCOhost, doi:10.1016/j.anifeedsci.2011.04.074.

Pietrykowski, Bruce. "You Are What You Eat: The Social Economy of the Slow Food Movement." Review of Social Economy, vol. 62, no. 3, 2004, pp. 307–21. JSTOR.

Reese, Ryan F., and Jane E. Myers. "EcoWellness: The Missing Factor in Holistic Wellness Models." Journal of Counseling & Development, vol. 90, no. 4, 2012, pp. 400–06. Wiley Online Library, doi:10.1002/j.1556-6676.2012.00050.x.

Sakaguchi, Leo, et al. "Tackling the Issue of Food Waste in Restaurants: Options for Measurement Method, Reduction and Behavioral Change." Journal of Cleaner Production, vol. 180, Apr. 2018, pp. 430–36. ScienceDirect, doi:10.1016/j.jclepro.2017.12.136.

Sandford, Juliana. "Reduce, Reuse, Go Vegan." Penn Sustainability Review, vol. 1, no. 9, Feb. 2017, http://repository.upenn.edu/psr/vol1/iss9/3.

Savolaine, John, and Paul F. Granello. "The Function of Meaning and Purpose for Individual Well ness." The Journal of Humanistic Counseling, Education and Development, vol. 41, no. 2, 2002, pp. 178–89. Wiley Online Library, doi:10.1002/j.2164-490X.2002.tb00141.x.

Snowdon, D. A. "Animal Product Consumption and Mortality Because of All Causes Combined, Coronary Heart Disease, Stroke, Diabetes, and Cancer in Seventh-Day Adventists." The American Journal of Clinical Nutrition, vol. 48, no. 3, Sept. 1988, pp. 739–48, doi:10.1093/ajcn/48.3.739.

Ting, Sarah. The Right to a Living Wage for Restaurant Workers. p. 4.

Twine, Richard. "Vegan Killjoys at the Table—Contesting Happiness and Negotiating Rela tionships with Food Practices." Societies, vol. 4, no. 4, Dec. 2014, pp. 623–39. www.mdpi. com, doi:10.3390/soc4040623.

Vallianatos, Mark, et al. "Food Access, Availability, and Affordability in 3 Los Angeles Commu nities, Project CAFE, 2004-2006." Preventing Chronic Disease, vol. 7, no. 2, Feb. 2010. Pu bMed Central, https://www.ncbi.nlm.nih.gov/pmc/articles/PMC2831781/.

Newspaper Articles

Flanders, Laura. "Serving up Justice." Nation, 2 Sept. 2013, pp. 22–26.

"RESPECT: Social Justice for Social Change." UWIRE Text, 2016.

Podcasts

Dillion, Julie. The Love Food Podcast.

Ho, Soleil, et al. The Racist Sandwich.

Knight, Dr. Phil, and Gerry Brisson. Food For Thought.

Meyncke, Amanda. Happiness Spells.

Wood Nickerson, Brittany. Thyme Herbal.

Thesis

Hambridge, Amy. The Attitude of Gratitude: A Guide to Finding Happiness through Food, Farms, and Family. https://compass.fivecolleges.edu/islandora/object/hampshire:1519. Accessed 25 Mar. 2019.

Web Pages

12 Dimensions of Wellness. http://www.wellpeople.com/WellnessDimensions.aspx?Sc=0. Ac cessed 22 Mar. 2019.

All About Environmental Eating: Part 2 | Precision Nutrition. https://www.precisionnutrition.com/aa-environmental-eating-2. Accessed 24 Mar. 2019.

Banschick, Mark. "The Sincerest Love - The Love for Food." Psychology Today, http://www.psychologytoday.com/blog/the-intelligent-divorce/201310/the-sincerest-love-the-love-food. Accessed 10 Feb. 2019.

Chicken Pot Pie Turnovers Recipe | Melissa d'Arabian | Food Network. https://www.foodnetwork.com/recipes/melissa-darabian/chicken-pot-pie-turnovers-recipe-1924003. Accessed 18 Nov. 2019.

"Children Kids Kitchen Pizza Party." Aliexpress.Com, https://www.aliexpress.com/item/Children-Kids-Kitchen-Pizza-Party-Fast-Food-Slices-Cutting-Pretend-Play-Food-Toy/32914970248.html?src=ibdm_d03p0558e02r02&sk=&aff_platform=&aff_trace_key=&af=&cv=&cn=&dp=. Accessed 1 Apr. 2019.

Grilled Salmon Sushi-Rice Bowl Recipe | Food Network. https://www.foodnetwork.com/recipes/grilled-salmon-sushi-rice-bowl-recipe-1944217. Accessed 14 Nov. 2019.

Hand Roll - Yelp. https://www.yelp.com/biz_photos/sushi-sasabune-honolulu?select=8KftcfWzFXK-x37r7y4D8g. Accessed 9 Mar. 2019.

"How Food And Relationships Are Linked In The Brain." HuffPost, 6 Jan. 2013, https://www.huffingtonpost.com/2013/01/06/food-and-love_n_2410936.html.

Thank You

I am eternally grateful to everyone who has helped bring my book to life. Without you, this dream would not have become a reality. I want to give special thanks to:

Mom
I don't know where I'd be without you. Without knowing it, you have been my inspiration in all my culinary adventures. You always allowed me to use our home kitchen as I please. You allowed my curiousity to thrive in all forms, encouraging me to try new things all the time.

My Division III Committee-Sarah Hews and John Castorino
This has been a wonderfully unexpected journey for the three of us. You've helped shape this book in so many different ways. While I had sad events occur in my personal life, you allowed me to take the time and space I needed to step away from my work and heal my heart, even when I didn't allow myself to do so. When I was hard on myself for having my heart guide my work, you reminded me this is not the end but only the beginning.

Seeta Sistla and Chris Cianfrani
You have both been there for me from the very beginning. A fearful first year student, anxious to change tutorials, you welcomed me to yours with open arms. You showed me the way and were there for me with every tense email. You reminded me to breathe and remember why I am here in times I needed it most. Your peaceful ways have stuck in the back of my mind everyday.

The Admissions Office
Other students find homes in student clubs and different Schools of Thought but I've found my home with you. Even when I didn't feel welcome in my own living situation, I felt welcome with you. You've been my friends, mentors, and most of all, you have been my family and I cannot thank you enough.

Author House Publishing
Since I was a child, it has been on my bucket list to publish a cookbook before I turn 30 years old. I can now say I published my first cookbook before I turned 22 years old! You have all been so wonderful to work with. I appreciate all you've done for me. Thank you.

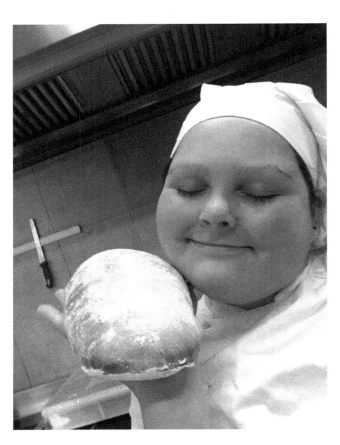

Chef, Artist, Activist

Carrie Jones Faina

Carrie is a Hampshire College graduate who studied Culinary Arts as a medium to connect social change, environmental justice, wellness, and visual arts. She has shown her interest in food, people, and the planet from the time she was a young child. She hopes to open a restaurant which fights for the health of the planet and food justice. As an undergraduate student, she studied abroad for a semester at Apicius International School of Hospitality in Florence, Italy. When Carrie is not cooking, she can be found eating delicious foods and exploring isles of the grocery store.